# JING AND THE

## Lunar New Year Lanterns

Jing
And the Lunar
New Year Lanterns
By KeriAnne Jelinek

It was the eve of Lunar New Year, and the village was alive with twinkling lanterns and the scent of dumplings.

Red banners fluttered in the breeze, carrying wishes of happiness and good luck.

LUNAR NEW YEAR

Amid the bustling streets, two children, Mei and Lin, peeked into their grandmother s workshop. Their eyes widened as they saw the most beautiful red dragon puppet with shimmering golden scales.

'Meet Jing," said Grandma, holding up the puppet. 'He will lead the Lunar New Year parade!"

'But Jing isn t real," Mei whispered. 'How will he bring the parade to life?"

Grandma smiled mysteriously. 'Dragons have a way of surprising you, my dear."

That night, Mei and Lin placed Jing
carefully by the window, letting
moonlight bathe his brilliant red scales.

Beside them sat Snowball, their fluffy
white cat. Snowball purred softly as if
he, too, was waiting for something
magical to happen.

Suddenly, a breeze swept through the room, rustling the lanterns. Jing s golden eyes glimmered.

'Did he just blink?" Lin asked, clutching Mei s arm.

Before they could answer, Jing stretched, yawned, and whoosh! His puppet strings disappeared, and he stood tall  a magnificent, living dragon!

'Children of the village," Jing said, his voice deep and warm, 'the Lunar New Year parade must begin at sunrise, but the lanterns are scattered across the hills. Without them, the celebration cannot light up the night sky."

'We ll help you find them!" Mei declared.

Jing s golden eyes twinkled. 'Climb aboard. And bring your brave little cat."

Snowball leapt onto Jing s back as Mei and Lin climbed up, holding tight to his silky red scales.

'Hold on!" Jing roared. With a flick of his tail, he soared into the starry sky.

High above the village, Jing flew toward the hills. The first lantern dangled from a tree branch. It shimmered like a tiny sun.

"I ll get it!" Mei cried, sliding down Jing s tail and scampering to the tree.

"Be careful!" Lin called.

Just as Mei reached for the lantern, a gust of wind blew it higher into the branches.

Snowball leapt gracefully from Jing s back, climbing the tree with ease. She batted the lantern down, and Lin caught it.

"One lantern down!" Mei cheered.

Deeper into the hills, they found a cluster of lanterns tangled in a thorny bush.

"Let me try," Mei said. She carefully untangled the red strings while Jing shielded her from the thorns with his wings.

As Mei freed the last lantern, a family of rabbits hopped out from the bush, their white fur dusted with gold.

"Happy New Year!" they squeaked. "We ll join the parade!"

The sky began to lighten, and the children
hurried to gather the last lantern, which
floated on a shimmering lake.

"How will we reach it?" Lin asked.

Jing s long tail dipped into the water, creating
gentle ripples. Snowball balanced on Jing s tail
like a tightrope walker, her white fur glowing
in the dawn. With a nimble leap, she snagged
the lantern and carried it back.

"Good kitty!" Mei laughed, hugging Snowball.

With the lanterns gathered, Jing roared triumphantly and flew back to the village just as the first rays of the sun peeked over the mountains.

The villagers gasped as they saw Jing carrying the glowing lanterns. He wove through the streets, his golden scales sparkling like firecrackers.

The rabbits hopped alongside, carrying
small lanterns.

Snowball perched proudly on Jing s head,
her tail swishing in time with the drums.

As the parade ended, Jing landed gently in front of Grandma s workshop.

"Thank you, children," Jing said, his golden eyes warm. "You have made this the brightest Lunar New Year."

With a flick of his tail, Jing transformed back into the puppet. Snowball nuzzled his side, purring softly.

Grandma appeared, her eyes twinkling. "Dragons always have a way of bringing people together," she said.

Mei and Lin smiled, knowing the magic of Jing would stay with them forever.

Under the glow of the lanterns, the village celebrated  a night filled with laughter, joy, and the promise of a bright new year.

As the parade ended, Jing landed gently
in front of Grandma s workshop.

"Thank you, children," Jing said, his
golden eyes warm. "You have made this
the brightest Lunar New Year."

With a flick of his tail, Jing transformed
back into the puppet. Snowball nuzzled
his side, purring softly.

Grandma appeared, her eyes twinkling. "Dragons always have a way of bringing people together," she said.

Mei and Lin smiled, knowing the magic of Jing would stay with them forever.

Under the glow of the lanterns, the village celebrated  a night filled with laughter, joy, and the promise of a bright new year.

www.ingramcontent.com/pod-product-compliance
Lightning Source LLC
LaVergne TN
LVHW070016220726
843921LV00002B/6